VIEWS FROM A

FERRIS

WHEEL

Poems by Robert Wallace

VIEWS FROM A
FERRIS
WHEEL

E. P. DUTTON & CO., INC. / NEW YORK 1965

Published simultaneously in Canada by Clarke, Irwin & Company Limited,
Toronto and Vancouver

Library of Congress Catalog Card Number: 65-19960

Some of these poems have appeared in periodicals, to whose editors I
make grateful acknowledgment, as follows:

THE ANTIOCH REVIEW: "Total" (1964)
APPROACH: "The House" (1965)
THE ATLANTIC MONTHLY: from "The Dictionary Zoo" ("Walrus," "Brontosaurus,"
    "Dromedary," "Gargoyle") (1960); "The Poet, Forsaken in Love, Is Visited at a
    Green Lake" (1963, as "Forsaken")
BEST ARTICLES AND STORIES: "The Kite" (reprint: 1960)
BOTTEGHE OSCURE: "Poem" (1955)
CAPE ROCK QUARTERLY: "Omen" (1965); "What He Says" (1965); "Ghosts"
    (1965)
CHICAGO REVIEW: "The Two Roads" (1961)
CHOICE: "Return" (1961)
THE CHRISTIAN SCIENCE MONITOR: "Adagio" (1953); "Out of the Window in De-
    cember" (1958)
THE COLORADO QUARTERLY: "The Kite" (1959)
EPOCH: "The Two Old Gentlemen" (1961); "Spring" (1965)
HARPER'S MAGAZINE: "In a Spring Still Not Written Of" (1965)
THE KENYON REVIEW: "A Sight of the Negro Funeral" (1964)
THE LADIES' HOME JOURNAL: "A Charm on Her Behalf" (© 1963 by The Curtis
    Publishing Company)

THE MASSACHUSETTS REVIEW: "Noon Photographs" (1961, as "Seven Noon Photographs"); "Under the September Peach" (1963); "Encounter" (1963); "Single, the Poet Is Surprised by Her Fever" (1963); "In the Shadows of Early Sunlight" (1963); "Nuns by the Sea" (1964)

THE NATION: "Fifteen Dolphins" (1963)

THE NEW YORKER: "Landscapes and Windows" (1955); "One January" (1956); "The Crayfish" (1956); "The Garden Snail" (1956); "The Mammoth" (1957); "A Problem in History" (1957); "The Star-Nosed Mole" (1960); "The Dictionary Ounce" (1961); "The Storm" (1964), © in the years indicated by The New Yorker Magazine, Inc.

THE NEW YORK HERALD TRIBUNE: "O Bright Two" (1956)

POETRY: "The Double Play" (1961); "A Snapshot for Miss Bricka Who Lost in the Semifinal Round of the Pennsylvania Lawn Tennis Tournament at Haverford, July, 1960" (1961); "A Last Photograph, for Being Divorced" (1965); "Instructions for Keeping a Muse" (1965), © in the years indicated by The Modern Poetry Association.

POETRY NORTHWEST: "A Love Poem—Probably" (1965)

QUEEN'S QUARTERLY: "Municipal Parking Lot" (1962, in a somewhat different version)

A REVIEW OF ENGLISH LITERATURE: "Saturday Movie" (1961)

THE SATURDAY REVIEW: "The White Crayfish" (1957)

SHENANDOAH: "Hail and Farewell" (1962, as "Ave Atque Vale"); "Manifesto for a Little Brass Key" (1965)

THE SOUTHERN REVIEW: "It Was the Sun" (1965); "The Noise That Woke Me Strangely" (1965)

TRANSATLANTIC REVIEW: "Above the River Country" (1962); "Girl in Front of the Bank" (1965)

THE VIRGINIA QUARTERLY REVIEW: "First Dandelions" (1960); "The Dark Burning" (1960); "Closing Down" (1964); "Data To Be Left in the Ruins" (1964)

THE WORMWOOD REVIEW: "Love Song at the Olivetti on Fifth Avenue" (1965)

Thirteen poems are reprinted from *This Various World and Other Poems*, Charles Scribner's Sons, *Poets of Today IV*, 1957.

The creatures of "The Dictionary Zoo" may be found in the pages of *The American College Dictionary*.

she knows,
for whom this book is

Contents

I

II

III

Up, up, we grind from down,
Rising on views of the town,
Circling above the trees'
Eye-splashing, level seas
On which roofs float, stacks, spires,
And silvery water-towers
Tilt like buoys. Thus all goes
Rounding, neither so low
We're only where we are
Nor, high, so high or far
As turns the varied landscape
Abstractly to a map:
Enough to let the strange
And the familiar exchange
Aspects, so both surprise us.
O up! the wheeling rises,
Over, and down, and around—
Until the accepted town
Shows the wonder that it is,
The world come new in this,
Its staleness gone, made sweet,
When we are back to feet.

I

The Storm

Noonlight is sudden-full of the spirits
of dead butterflies, moving
—like a holiday!
surely, all that have ever been!
They are like flowers in the bushy pine,
on hedges, trees; fluttering
knee-deep in the fields; flailing
out of a sky thick with them as if with snow.
I go up on the roof to see them.
The landscape is a blizzard of hues,
farms going under,
—wingbeats, petals, flakes—
they come in at my lips and eyelids,
they fly in the currents of my blood;
friendly, they kill with such gentle wings,
knives stroking as softly as eyelashes.
The day hums in their overshadowings
—they will cover the electric lines;
even the mountains will be buried
in this colored Pompeii,
in these deep, bright ashes.

The Noise That Woke Me Strangely

was my neighbor chopping wood at midnight.
The floodlight, from his porch, made him a shadow
dancing over a larger shadow dancing
crazily about him, arms and all angles
where the frame house cornered into shrubby dark.
He laid on stroke, and stroke, and stroke. The grass
of summer shone a fierce and April green
in the light's ellipse; the axe, about his head,
darted like a bird startled from its sleep,
and couldn't leave the light alone. He seemed
a dark St. Francis preaching in a clearing
the animals came to. The axe chipped moths
up, where it worked, and scattered them like flowers
along the grass-top, or little funerals
floating upon a lightning-colored sea
that wouldn't sink them. The circle, darkness, might
have held adoring foxes from the wood,
owls studious of his passion in the trees,
hawks, sharp squirrels, deer dreaming of fangs,
field mice amazed, in tiny rows, and opossums
silvery like hairy moons that had learned teeth
and glittering eyes—all devil's creatures come,
assembled to see his midnight leaping. They—
if they were there, watching—they were unseen
or seen only in the force that swung the blade.
It was such work at least as men don't do
for need of wood, won't do if they can sleep,
on nights of open windows. The axe's *chonk, chonk,*
rang like a bell against the darkish hills,
and got an echo, a twin off in the woods
or Abel by some shadowy barn. Nothing showed
what anger or despair burned in his blood,
and put his hands like prayer upon the axe handle;

later, he never said it. But by morning,
whatever it was had left the little oak
in a thousand pieces, a stack of wood to burn
his voiceless rage into the winter nights—
smoke, drifting, and the faraway stars. His labor
was dark light. He flailed away. Whenever
it was, no one was watching when he stopped.
As always, in the morning, he waved cheerily
from his leafed garden as I drove, waving, past.

A Problem in History

At morning light the ark lay grounded fast
On' top of Ararat; and Noah sent out
The raven flapping on jet-fingered wings
Unreturning; and thrice to look about
Sent the timid dove, that returned at last
Fluttering an olive bough. The robin sings

On the spattered rail and the sun shines
On the steaming earth, that like a bog stank
Greening at the clear blue sky. Asses bray
From the hold, the animals come down the plank
By twos and twos, in awkward-footed lines
Sniffing, while hawks and songbirds spray

Into the new air. Forgetful of the flood,
In a busy hour all are debarked and gone
Down from Ararat. By sunfall the voices
Of their going have vanished. The ark alone
Centers their outward footprints in the mud,
Settles through the night with creaking noises

Wearied with its long journey. In that repose
New suns will wreathe it was green-ivy vines,
Shade it with growing oaks and bushes round
There on the world's top, till it rots with rains
And snows and suns of time. And no one knows
What green the unreturning raven found.

A Sight of the Negro Funeral

Leading, the hearse shrugged up onto the highway,
and shinnied off two hundred yards below
—where a little road accepted the way a woods
had curved, and strung its fence and begun to go

staggering up the long hill. Traffic swished by,
hard, and didn't let the small procession out,
its headlights shining in the stormy gloom
like animal eyes. The cars watched, dim, in doubt,

but one by one they turned, and turned off, and joined
the waiting hearse, smoking, beneath the oaks.
And then they started on. Their small dusts, rising,
the red lights pushing on and off, bespoke

the column, dipping, along the ruts and holes
toward what we could not see: the pine-roofed top
of a gray hill, the dismounted mourners halting
beside the long-grassed grave, the earth heaped up,

and all the singing. Four cars like a kite's tail
behind the hearse, old Chevies and a Ford,
they fluttered up where the land rose out of view,
carrying their flowery cargo toward their Lord

—vanished over. Thundering. The dark sky rained;
rained. We knew no more than that a man had died,
but we wished him, and all of them, better luck
than they were having on his last ride.

The Two Old Gentlemen

Though the house had burned years ago,
with everything in it,
all that had been brought out in the wagons,
all that had been added since,
the photographs, the pink-flowered paper,
the stuffed furniture from St. Louis,
the blue gilt set of Dickens their father
had ordered from the salesman out from St. Louis—

Though the house had burned years ago,
they always talked of it
and of the times there had been in it
when they were boys, before they were boys,
the uncle who had been wounded at Antietam
and had come west and died before they were born,
their mother churning on the porch, the arrowheads
they once found along the banks of the green creek—

Though the house had burned years ago,
with everything in it,
they sat talking, these childless gentlemen,
in the sun-high field where the hay was making,
these gentle children by the big red baler,
talking of Mr. Micawber and Little Nell,
of Dombey, and Krook who turned to smoke,
and Pickwick travelling the road to Norwich.

Total

Crossing Ohio, all of a July afternoon,
the turnpike
in sunlight before us, behind us,
we hit on 27 butterflies,
crushing against windshield and shiny steel.
White. Brown. Orange. Looping
easily out of the woods, off of the fields,
swallowtails, monarchs, lemon-wings, glass-wings, white
    cabbages,
into the stream of death.
Twenty-seven!

       East of Elyria,
one mottled wing
hung flapping to the glass terribly
before hurtling loose and
overhead;
mostly, however, they left colored stars,
nova-stains, against our racing sky.

It Was the Sun

that pulled the pine up to that ragged height,
and lit the simple blue behind it;
                    —but who decided on
(among that fierce, self-shadowed green)
a cardinal: his jewel's, heart's color?

A Snapshot for Miss Bricka Who Lost in the Semifinal Round of the Pennsylvania Lawn Tennis Tournament at Haverford, July, 1960

Applause flutters onto the open air
like starlings bursting from a frightened elm,
and swings away across the lawns
in the sun's green continuous calm

of far July. Coming off the court,
you drop your racket by the judge's tower
and towel your face, alone, looking off,
while someone whispers to the giggling winner,

and the crowd rustles, awning'd in tiers
or under umbrellas at court-end tables,
glittering like a carnival
against the mute distance of maples

along their strumming street beyond
the walls of afternoon. Bluely, loss
hurts in your eyes—not loss merely,
but seeing how everything is less

that seemed so much, how life moves on
past either defeat or victory,
how, too old to cry, you shall find steps
to turn away. Now others volley

behind you in the steady glare;
the crowd waits in its lazy revel,
holding whiskey sours, talking, pointing,
whose lives (like yours) will not unravel

to a backhand, a poem, or a sunrise,
though they may wish for it. The sun
brandishes softly his swords of light
on faces, grass, and sky. You'll win

hereafter, other days, when time
is kinder than this worn July
that keeps you like a snapshot: losing,
your eyes, once, made you beautiful.

The Double Play

In his sea-lit
distance, the pitcher winding
like a clock about to chime comes down with

the ball, hit
sharply, under the artificial
banks of arc lights, bounds like a vanishing string

over the green
to the shortstop magically
scoops to his right whirling above his invisible

shadows
in the dust redirects
its flight to the running poised second baseman

pirouettes
leaping, above the slide, to throw
from mid-air, across the colored tightened interval,

to the leaning-
out first baseman ends the dance
drawing it disappearing into his long brown glove

stretches. What
is too swift for deception
is final, lost, among the loosened figures

jogging off the field
(the pitcher walks), casual
in the space where the poem has happened.

Noon Photographs

I. A gold-black blossom of bees
　　swarms,
　　　　rustling like petals

in the breeze,
　　about the rotted eave
　　　　of the old garage.

Another,
　　at the corner where
　　　　the dirty yellow stucco

has fallen,
　　blooms
　　　　bright in the open lathwork.

II. A workman, an old man
　　with a rake
　　　　stands as if stunned,

red-faced in the heat,
　　by the bonfire
　　　　of July's dried-up breakage,

which, without flames,
　　burns
　　　　with heat shimmers in the light.

III. The eye
　　accepts
　　　　a green backdrop of oaks

and locusts, in whose shade
        dappled
                with light, sheets

and towels and shirts
        hang
                like the stilled

banners
        of a strange and distant
                morning.

IV. Voices
        from beyond the lilac hedge
                carry

in the still air. They tell,
        with their shrill flowings
                and fadings,

like a weather vane,
        which way the wind
                leans.

V. At a far sound
        the white-and-brown terrier
                rises

faunlike,
        ears erect,
                listening

through the still sunlight,
        looking
                toward the distant

29

buildings. Then, again,
  lies
    flat in the clovered grass.

VI. The boy in shade-green shorts
  and red
    canvas shoes, cries

 where he has fallen by the sandbox
  wall,
    amid his colored trucks.

 Overhead in the sun
  the sky
    looms, hot and blue.

VII. In the sun a tiny
  white
    butterfly

 skitters
  abstractedly
    above the grass,

 lights,
  skitters again till the eye loses hold,
    and

 carrying his journey with him
  is
    gone.

Fifteen Dolphins

Fifteen dolphins in procession,
parallel to the beach,
stitch with their gray the blue ocean,
sliding, diving leisurely in the Atlantic, rising
leisurely ahead, slow-motioning over
in the sea's peaked roofs.
                                   Among umbrellas
we stand, climb on chairs, shading eyes
to see their casual progression
past the beach, as if they were old gods,
as if we believed in what we cannot know,
the windowless water and the wind
running on the sea's thatch, before us.

Landscape and Windows

From the train, this green countryside under a blue lake
Of rippling sky, poplars washing green and white
In the wind, and nobody travelling
The brown river of road unravelling
Toward distant spires. The July bright

Sun beams bewilderingly on nothing; nothing
Stirs but the wind high up, and the eye
Follows the seams of the woven wheat, cool green
Light from the lake's demesnes,
And the eye wonders and never questions why

Or how such formal beauty gathers, carelessly.
But in Sainte Chapelle the eye wants reasons
For such walls of broken, glittering lights,
A muchness of many-colored delight,
Finds beauty the same under every sky and season,

Whether sun or snow lies heaped on Paris rooftops.
Behind the light of this colored-glass wilderness
The eye sees fingers, brown and cracked
Move with a stiff awkward tact,
Assembling the pieces of too much loveliness.

Adagio

Old kings of China riding
On golden plumed white asses,
That toil up, slightly nodding,
Through rocky mountain-passes,
In the bright and glass-blue weather,
Old kings of China riding
In a white and golden line.

Up past the berry bushes
And the white-bark elms they go,
Beyond the rivers' splashes,
And the summits' glistering snow,
In the bright and glass-blue weather,
Old kings of China riding
In a white and golden line.

They go riding, riding, high
In an endless slow procession
From the mountains through the sky,
Riding slowly to the sun,
In the bright and glass-blue weather,
Old kings of China riding
In a white and golden line.

The bright twin rails
     curve
          into view,

and arrowing through
     greenness,
          tie by tie,

shape the summer earth
     to purpose, linking
          distances and

distances.
     A hawk
          rides his

own
     flitting shadow
          over the fenced cornfield

and weeds and
     gravel
          of the high embankment

and away to the southeast.
     The rails
          glitter; bare-shouldered, a boy

walks
     along them in the sun.
          The wild

blackberries
        trail
                by the tracks

where the woods begin.
        The silver-painted signal
                arm

shows a green
        eye,
                beckoning

departures.
        And
                under the trestle

the creek
        drifts;
                it is summer in the new world.

It is
        burning
                noon when the freight

swings
        unseeing
                in its trestled stride

over the
        green country creek,
                which

has no nymph
        in
                misted chronicle,

but has a boy
    appearing
        and disappearing

in the green
    deep
        water in the sunlight.

Poem

Sunny in the distance by the hills
                     a long freight
Rumbles, the low rhythmic clang
And wheeze of couplings, and smoke
                 in the bright still air;

Nearer, in the field, a white
                  butterfly, poised
On the warm rough handle,
Rides lazily the slow swirls
                 of an old man's hoe.

And far off Odysseus returning,
                   the wine-dark sea
Furrowing under the straight keel,
Glittering in the silence of the sun,
                 Odysseus returning.

And the freight rumbles in the strange
                 land, and the sea
Sparkles and furls to the purring keel,
And an old man hoes in the field,
                 in the silence of the sun.

A Love Poem—Probably

A huge moth sleeps against my ceiling.
You will laugh if I tell you,
or put him into a poem
—huge, with huge wings of mottled browns
like dust, circled,
in which rain has fallen.

I did not invent him;
the painters left the screens down
and the windows wide to the night air.
I cannot hear his breathing
—huge, antennaed in the dark,
he grows to the shapes of all shadows.

Since you will not love me,
nor believe me,
and can go from me so easily,
I will not say who this terrible fellow is—
unmoved in the night—who
shares the ceiling I sleep on.

The Older Man's Song

The shale cliff edge gives in.
Year by year the locust
she played beneath as a child,
slowly sinks and tilts
outward, gone twelve feet down;
its roots hang half in air,
though still it manages green.
What will become of a man
who wants to love a girl?

A storm will bring it down.
It will stand upside down
in sand, on the narrow shoal,
upon its two forked limbs,
in water to woody ankles.
Its roots will open like hair.
What will become of a man
who wants to love a girl?

One spring it won't be there,
but will have walked on out
in the lake's eight hundred feet,
dragging with it the fence
she played in as a child
that bends and sags, too, and will fall.
What will become of a man
who wants to love a girl?

Data To Be Left in the Ruins

I let the puppy chew an old
house-painting loafer, dotted in as many colors
as a trout—whose shape it mimics, too,
hung from a crossed knee, fighting a current
of playfulness.
                    September has collapsed,
like an old empire. The golden air
is all October, ruin; the sun rides chill
for all its watery brightnesses,
the trees that wall the north gully
rustle with reds,
yellows, with greens darker than summer's
belonging to the pines, pecans. Spines
of onion grass, now we have stopped
mowing for the season, march leggily to a wind
I cannot hear.
                    Perhaps the air
carries news out of worn Zimbabwe,
or of the ruined Dzata, or of those cities
whose piled stones melt into jungles
on the plateaus above the Orinoco.
It has scarved ruins, this air, at least—dissolving,
or dark in the sea.
                    I am no alarmist;
it is only hard to say these shadows
belong only to the season, to say the air
rings with nothing.
                    Going off, in jumps,
the puppy travels sideways, stumbling,
stringing distances like lines across
the light, the little rises of the lawn.

Closing Down

Through rinsing the car for the last time
before winter, I broke up the hose
and coiled its sections, stiff with summer,
and carried them one by one through
the three-foot-high plank door leading
under one corner of the house, into
a shallow dirt-floored place of boards
old buckets bicycle wheels poles shingles,
piled and cluttered. The light followed
me in. Through the door the world
was like a sullen photograph
I climbed back into, going out;
the crab grass, lacking its one last mowing,
seemed a junkyard of ruined antennae
below the sagging pear tree's fountain,
to the crawling eye. I hung the hoses
from back-wall hooks. On the final trip,
I came with pliers to reach among
the ghostly cobwebs and shut off
the pipe that runs along the rafters
to outside, and open the copper cock
that lets the water guzzle from the pipe.
I had gone, hunched like a queer spider,
in and out the tiny door; when I stood
again, at last, upright in the air,
the painty hook forced in on darkness,
I was surprised I had not closed
October down. The pine rose still
green-fired in the tall sky, the gold fields
rode still moored in the lines of light
like a fleet rocking with all arrivals.
I stood, among my sponges and bucket,
amazed, like a tiny Gulliver,
at how huge and shining the broad world was.

The Dark Burning

This
          báckyard bonfire, at my poking,
                    fires

its own
          orange
                    stars

up in the darkening November night,
          swirling
                    dusts

of tiny lights, bright
          and climbing,
                    by the wire fence

out back of the garage. Dry
          leaves,
                    and a crumpled

branch of the dogwood
          burn
                    into these stars,

a cardboard box of wood scraps,
          some
                    old newspapers

flaming
          with their old wars,
                    triumphs,

used-up disasters,
    and a brown sack
        of paper-trash (waste

bits
    of all our lovings,
        livings,

dyings—broken
    poems,
        bills, letters

never now to be answered,
    dog-
        eared lists

of worn-out duties and desires)
    —all but what we go on keeping,
        cherish

for a slower, dimmer
    burning
        out. O here!

what bursts of stars!
    bright,
        roiling heavens

tended
    with a stick, swift
        galaxies! They

rise
    as
        if intent

on reaching more than treetops,
    out-
        reaching hope, upward

by the bare trees,
    as if swarming up
        toward Orion

or the shadowy Bear, as if
    at least
        to set one new star

off
    there in heaven,
        to mark

something
    gone
        out here in the earth's cold dark.

But O! they
    perish
        brightly, star by flashing star

fade,
    upward,
        spark

by dwindling spark,
    fail
        until the dark eye alone

climbs
    skyward
        to the frozen tracts

of heaven's stars,
　　which
　　　　burn in a hard light.

But burn, too!
　　burn
　　　　for all that icy glitter,

burn while
　　the fire goes black at my feet
　　　　and the earth,

turned
　　dark
　　　　behind my back, lies

still.
　　For
　　　　all stars burn,—

and everywhere,
　　raging,
　　　　as far as eye can see,

silent around me, wildly,
　　swift as loss,
　　　　the whole dark burning!

A Charm on Her Behalf

Thread, go straight to the needle's eye;
Keys, find keyholes in any dark;
Pins, do not prick her; nor, pencils, break—
For who's to praise, but you and me
Since sun's impartial, moon is cold,
And the stars are all sly and old?

Watches, tick gently to her ears
The endless riding of her years.

Keep carefully, books, her places;
And, glasses, travel safely in her hand;
Blow gently on her, wind;
Buttons, hold; and you, tiny laces—
For all loveliness at last goes whither
The flowers go, into death's weather.

Clocks, chime sweetly to her ears
The endless riding of her years.

Always attend her, oh, be tender,
Sweet ghostling daily things,
Teapot and soap and scissors and rings—
From all the harms you may, defend her
And make, of all your little ways,
A celebration of her days.

Out of the Window in December

In the blue and ceramic sunlight,
in air liquid
and flashing clear as spring water,

in the wind's strong weaving current,
a few curled
and brilliant paper-yellow leaves

in a thin and crooked tree struggle on
like minnows,
bright, twisting, frozen into glass.

Nuns by the Sea

(for Loren Oliver)

Now, in the dark of winter,
when the night's cold fills the house
in spite of thermostat, and the double-windows
runnel with a moonless dark that moves
upon the earth, lawns and fields,
and twins my bedded dark,
I remember the nuns swimming, in July,
at the far, other end of the year.

Wearing black tunics below the knees,
belted with white ropes,
and white or aqua bathing caps, they came;
in sneakers or matching rubber bathing shoes,
carrying towels, they came toward the sea
like birds fluttering in a strange plumage,
slowly, and eddied about a green table
and benches in the sand:
in little groups went toward the sea.

Mysterious to the summer, sand and waves,
they made a dark purpose
I walked beach miles to see,
leaning at last on a breakwater's stones and piers.
Their frugal colors seemed to warm
in the aching sun, in sand's glare,
and the buoyant waters bore
their floating tunics like elusive flowers
about them, shiny with wetness.

Fours and fives of them, in the surf,
made circles—holding hands,
surviving the waves' long rolling walls

tossed on them; dancing in the sea;
laughing, these black brides—
or in a huge comb, roaring about them,
they went over, black in the sea's white,
tumbled, until still holding hands
their fences rose up to pasture bits of the sea again.
Here and there, one drifted
in the glassy troughs; or, farther out, swam them
slowly with white arms rising like a team of swans
from a sunken, harnessed skiff.

The sun was lovely. They laughed
beneath the shell of sky
and, though the wind, offshore,
hid their voices, sang
—a school of mermaids, passing a spell
beyond the bright asperities of our colored beach,
our blankets, transistors, balls, and love—
their hidden voices sang
and clouds like feathers fell
across the sky and drifted, misting, out to sea.

Now, in the dark of winter,
in a house filled up with cold,
far, at the other end of the year,
I remember the nuns swimming, in July,
and see them in the lighted cave of the mind,
at a distance, all splashing
from the cold dark of their habits in the sun,
and hear more of their flutish voices, singing,
than I heard in the high summer
with my ear to the wind's shell,
when I saw them swimming beyond the naked sand,
birds, dark birds, dark flowers wetly
blossoming—in the high sun,
lovers, romping, practicing paradise.

II

Dust

The dust sprouts terribly in all my rooms.
Though the windows stay shut,
little animals of it
creep from under my bed, out of corners,
and leap about in the doorways
dancing to my passage.

                  For six weeks
I have been at poems, shuffling the pages,
talking to myself,
stitching the stiff ink-brocade, the scribbly worm-marks
of my wandering
from room to room.

              On the winter ledge
—on cold concrete, snow behind him—
a sparrow in his ruffly greatcoat,
the soul bright in his eyes' little windows,
seems attracted by the commotion.

The Star-Nosed Mole

Once neighbor to the dinosaur,
    dweller
        in the underground,

denizen of these old lands,
    swimmer
        in the earth, his element,

the star-nosed mole
    favors
        our fields and farms,

browses beneath the happy suburbs,
    persists
        along the netted runways

of his love and fear,
    sightless
        where the bright years pass

above him.
    Fierce
        in love and battle, little,

ungainly with his hidden ears,
    he forages
        the deep, rich country

of the dark. On his snout he bears
    before him,
        always, a naked fringe

of fleshy feelers, rose-colored,
    a star;
        a pugnacious flower of darkness,

travelling the hungry tunnels
    scooped
        by powerful claws,

active in all seasons,
    moving,
        at all hours searching

eyelessly for his endless dinner,
    star tentacles
        in constant motion—

lowly
    Arcturus,
        whose hunger is his twinkle.

Sometimes you will see him,
    in winter,
        emerge briefly from his tunnels

beneath the snow crust;
    blind
        and glossy, he comes a moment

out into the open sunlight,
    stands
        in all the brilliance he can see,

in the wind, and vanishes
    again
        into his darkling courses.

The Mammoth

The hulking mammoth steering
through the clearing

treads heavy-footed, tall;
the green wood's all

aglitter, flecks of sunlight
gleam, lying bright

as minted gold or glass
along the grass

the mammoth stalks. He moves
as it behooves

a wintry beast undone
with northward sun,

beset by too much spring—
huge, lumbering,

and slow. Wearing strangeness
and his winter dress

(that fringed with snow would pass
in icecap glass

for elegance at least),
he eyes with priest-

sad-look in either eye,
the burning sky,

the altered earth, and sees
through snow-filled trees

the icecap continent
of his intent.

And, turning, the mammoth goes
clumsy with woes,

shaggy, northward in search
of ice-bound birch

and pine, the glacial earth
that shaped his birth.

* * *

And if the mammoth chose
the polar snows,

and sank in gleaming mud
that glassed his blood

and froze his stride to stone,
crystal, alone,

or laid his hairy flank
against a bank

of sedgeless ice, and slept,
at least he kept

a faith learned at the knees
of ancient trees,

and found an icy range
beyond all change.

And if the bright green wood
the mammoth stood

strange in once, remains, know
all green woods go:

and earth will bring down twice
the moving ice

on lands of green and sun.
All deaths are one.

One for the Season

Senile, infinite Spring! Wanderer!
why do you offer us
all these bright trinkets?—birds, junk of tulips
or lilacs, glass beads on stems, gewgaws, green—
to the dying?
We are natives of
wherever you got them
—every opening of our eyes is pushing
earth-grains aside,
is the flowers' seeing.
We are the dying.
We come from there, old Spring!
wanderer—like Ponce de León
into this dangerous upper air.

First Dandelions

The sun hangs
medals,
    bright, pompous, golden
       medals

on the grass,
    which
       stands

green and tall
    in a million,
       million

ranks across the yard.
    A dew-starred
       bluet

rustles a command;
    a jay screams.
       A

flight of sparrows roars
    over,
       dipping,

to the east;
    and
       somewhere

a screen door bangs
    a
       brisk
and ceremonial salute!

Spring

Soon, the poison ivy will learn green
and loose its pennants from (unseen)

its dark headquarters—tendrils rising
in the general botanizing,

fluttering through the field-grass spears
like flags of battle. Evil appears

always in the colors of the good:
as this will, in lawn, garden, wood,

by the lake, the road, wherever I pass
or my dogs run in lanes or grass.

Soon, stirring, the bitter, pretty leaves
of love that my dark heart conceives

will flutter up, subversive banners
shaking the wind, so that a man errs

into every poisonous patch. Sun, showers
will see the joined and armied hours

marching on bloom. And by mid-May
I'll wear the frothy flowers, the gay

and reddish wounds of ivy, love,
these wars I'm always veteran of.

To a Monarch Butterfly Blown Seventeen Miles to Sea
epithalamium: L. and M. J.

Reckless voyager, had you a cry
and/or I

the minimal ear
to hear

it, in this round, immense
silence

of sunny blues, sloshing, dry,
sea, sky,

you might say what started you hither,
whether

a lonely choice or (as I guess)
only

a too-strong wind, and say what small passion
drives you on

this far from the gardeny land.
But here you stand,

resting on a tiny boat hardly
afloat

itself amid this barren, glass
Sahara's

bottle-blue: on a coiled rope silent,
wings bent

and rusty from the blowy sky,
awry,

slowly fanning as if they were
breathing,

but, oh, you're flower-casual, stiff,
as if

unwilling to admit doubt, self-
pity,

or anybody's question. Then off,
aloft,

a fluttering hurled in the wind,
high over the world

again, trackless, beating eastward, a small
backward

Columbus, sure to fall before
Por-

tugal. O tiny adventurer vanishing
in the sky,

I am as lost in these blue
woods as you,

but have not found so straight
or true a way

—when all the tall winds are blowing—
of going on.

To a Bird Watcher, but Gratefully

They are Arctic terns I watched all summer,
you tell me
: flat-black-capped, with pointy wings,
above the salt marsh or like a plummet dropping
into the inlet and emerging
from the splash, swimming into the air,
a minnow crosswise in the beak.

The crested fellow that obligingly came
to the window, despite binoculars,
and so was named, is a kingfisher.

The white ones in the marsh are egrets,
not herons,
in the crusty wind-row cedars.

That much for sure, though the sandpipers
that rolled in a row
before a wave up the beach might have been
Baird's or White-rumped, or some other,
for all of Roger Tory Peterson.

                        Anyway,
it is good to be less ignorant
of their names than I was, or than they are.

Mosquitoes

Into the room,
a salty-screened dark of shore cottage,
against the fastnesses of sleep
they come
. . . tiny, ancient Luftwaffe of the night,
circling, whining,
down
—zingling
at my ear: at which I throw
slapped hands
up like flak, bursts of random hate
popping among them,
over the pillows, as they dive,
and, on
elbows, snap the light
on—glaring, the searchlight of will—;
and, one by one,
slowed to themselves in air, flimsy
machines of line,
they fall,
or crash against the painted sky
—contraptions, bloodied, fine as hair—:
the Black
Ace drops, the Knight of Death smashes
to the mirror,
blind Baron X hangs like a permanent star, &
the Dark Lady spins
lightly
to the landscape of the bed:
until, by so many victories,
—queer as old newsreels to memory—
the rich city

of the blood at last may sleep defended,
dreaming,
as the cool moon rises
outside the screens, and glints on the peaceful waters.

At seven, on the dock next door,
    father and son
        clump on the boards, lift

and turn
    a rusty oil-drum
        out of which pour fish (mostly

blues) into a shiny heap.
    They
        hose them down. Seeing

us on our elbows in the window,
    the father calls,
        "Hundred and fifty!"

as the water splashes his trousers.
    We wave.
        We are first to get the news.

from The Dictionary Zoo

I. THE WALRUS

Looking like 1905,
though considerably older,
obviously longing to wive
and sport where the air is apt to be colder

than here, the walrus sits
between Walpurgis Night and waltz,
nicely suspended between the flesh's and the spirit's
comfortable faults,

but ignoring both, looking straight ahead,
a dreamy lounger in the Arctic sun,
fin-feet spread,
exile from the blizzard coasts where ice floes run;

(1/120) natural size,
the leathery whale-horse (from the Dutch),
by the look in his heavy-lidded eyes,
doesn't like it much.

II. THE BRONTOSAURUS

Thunder-lizard (Greek) and huge as you want, he's
    really
            well-meaning
                    and kind—
though clumsy, a nibbler of grass and of leaves,
    with a tiny,
            prehistoric
                    mind.

Next door neighbor here and now to the Brontës,
    Emily
        and Charlotte
        and Anne,
the slow-witted brontosaurus behaves
    as well
        as he possibly
            can.

III. THE GARGOYLE

The gargoyle is a bird of stone
    who never flaps his wings,
and is (Old French *gargouille*) mostly throat.

Though strong and fierce, he has never flown;
    but nests on roofs, and clings
to cornices, high and remote.

The gargoyle perches all alone,
    and when it rains, he sings—
a gurgle is his single note.

IV. THE DROMEDARY

The wary dromedary,
one-humped, solitary

on the page,
    seems disposed
        (though named from the Greek for the way he can sprint)

to be stationary
here, never to carry

a desert load again.
   He looks
      quite secretly pleased to be in print;

his mien is so very
aloofly, assuredly merry.

V. THE OUNCE

The spotted, whiskered, feline ounce
is not about to pounce

on some unsuspecting reader's blouse or vest.
Merely, he is depressed.

The mood is printed clearly in his face:
he's all upset about the narrow space

he's been assigned
and the way he's been defined—

always to be a second meaning,
always to have to crouch, leaning,

under a ledge of text,
annexed

to a puny unit of weight,
is sad enough for anybody's fate,

but it must be especially hard
for a snowy leopard,

accustomed to far Siberian peaks.
His gaze bespeaks

the plight of one who, having a lovely tail, is having to sit
on it

looking glumly off the page
in far too short and low a cage.

The Crayfish

I.

The brook wound through the woods behind
The houses, on each trim side was lined

With a wall of orange-brown rocks.
There, I sat with my shoes and socks

Off, under the tall oaks on the bank,
And dangled a piece of string that sank

Its load of bacon slowly down
To the dusty bottom. No sound

Ruffled the water, when I saw
A big crayfish stepping near the raw

Bait. I moved the string to inform
Him of it—back he leaped in a storm

Of cloudy mud. But soon he returned
Clumsy to eat what he had learned

Was easy lunch. He paused to fondle
The soggy dish, then like a bundle

Took it in his heavy pincers. Up,
Up, carefully I drew him up,

Dripping, through his watery sky,
Into my world of green and dry.

II.

He started off with a waddling walk
From the ledge, but wanting to talk

I set him back. So he sat there,
His black-reflector eyes in a stare

Of strangeness, while I told and told
How I was a boy, was nine years old,

And liked him. He swayed his feelers round
To show attention at the sound

I made, in the hollow glade of noon.
Wet slow scrapings were all the tune

His clumsy pincers could provide
For answer. I stroked his armored side,

Brown with yellow speckles like hail
In a dry garden, his plated tail

With its fan-feather-tips, his spiny
Spider-legs (one missing): my tiny

Monster from the stream. And to show
How well I liked him I let him go.

III.

I dropped him back with a soft splash
To catch again, and in a flash

He shot away in his liquid world
Between two rocks. Slowly I unfurled

My string, and let the tattered bait
Down into his sky again, to wait

On the dusty bottom. The string
Sent wrinkles out in widening rings,

That touched against the wall to go
Sliding back like messengers to and fro,

To confuse the sun. Mottled in shade
And sun the stream moved its slow parade

Between the walls; the watery bed
Lay like a desert rock-strewn and dead

Around my line. I'd thought to hoist
My brown acquaintance up from his moist

Nook beneath the rocks, to let him eat
The bacon as a friendly treat.

Below, I could see his pointed snout
Watching, but nothing would coax him out

To ride again up the sunny air.
I had to go and leave him there.

The Garden Snail

This backyard
    cousin
        to the octopus

Sees
    through two filmy
        stems

On his head, at
    need
        can peer round

Corners, and
    so betrays his
        huge

Timidity. He
    moves on his
        single

Elastic foot
    seldom,
        preferring

Anonymity
    to danger,
        seems

Often to be
    meditating
        a very tough

Problem, likes
    green leaves
        and water.

Shyness
    is his prime
        virtue,

Though I have seen
    one,
        on a blue day

In summer,
    go climbing
        all afternoon

With his brown shell
    up the wobbly tall
        grass,

For a good
    look-round
        at the wide world.

The White Crayfish

> *The light which puts out our*
> *eyes is darkness to us.*
> —Thoreau

The white crayfish lives in a cave
in utter darkness save

for the feeble yellow beam
turned into the stream,

which shows back surprise
in a thousand eyes

but runs on darkling clear
as twinkling glass. Here,

beneath the root-bearded sky,
miles or inches high,

where the stream unseeing mulls
the shining pebbles

in its mind, the silent crayfish
in darkling wish

sits ivoried and wholly still
in the current's will,

one tiny heavy pincer lost,
a kind of armored ghost,

whose feelers slightly bend
in the liquid wind

the water is moving in his world.
His eyes are pearled,

cloudy and hard—useless
when strangely thus

exposed to light—though may it be
they sometimes see

the dark itself, the figures of it,
and show back, darkly, wit?

They show no special interest in
a kindly-meaning sun,

preferring dark to all the light
they've ever seen, or might.

A delicate star assembles high
in the hairy sky,

a shining water beadlet, drops,
tattering the water-top

like web-cracked window glass
and swiftly passes

seaward into dark, leaving the stream
as it had been

save for the mirrored vanishing
and backward spring

of the crayfish, who elsewhere
now in the clear

and watery dark sits motionless,
knowing what we only guess,

that dark has stars that slowly fall
but is as good, withal,

as light. Both running stream and crayfish in their ways,

though dark as perfect night, conceal
what light reveals,

and lightless make a light reply.
In dark, stars die,

and dark is all the same as light,
if you see it right.

Manifesto for a Little Brass Key

I found it
once in deep grass where it shone

from the vertical shadows, brushing it
free of leaf-stuff, grass bits,

the colors of the sun—
tiny, tuneful, for locking and unlocking nothing,

ringing it among all the practical keys
of my life

that let me enter the places I am known
—look, who am I to say

there isn't a door it was meant for
opening, into love

or money or some other good thing:
and I'll go through.

Single, the Poet Is Surprised by Her Fever

Helplessly as a hospital father I make faces
into the darkened drugstore glass until
the pharmacist takes pity, turns the key
(already in the lock, dangling) and lets me in
among the shadowy bottles, shelves, bargains,
lit balefully by one light at the back.
He is patient in spectacles; I do dizzily
my errand. And I am strangely joyful, emerging
with ice cream, book, thermometer in a bag
to find my way (wishing for flowers
at midnight) through streets tunneled in the stars
to you, to stand, to be the fever's father,
cheerful, gay, loving your fierce-sweet child.

The Poet, Forsaken in Love, Is Visited at a Green Lake by His Good Angel Who Determines Him Wisely

Into my deep sadness came he bouncing
from the woods—a slate-blue butterfly
with a thread of crimson on each wing,
flittering on the weathered dock-boards
like a pennant windy with the most cheerful news.

He fluttered about me, dime-tinier,
merry as money, perching on knees
as if they were gay as Noah's mountain,
lighting among my upturned toes
as if for sweetnesses, as if they were good flowers

—until I have understood his coming!
Though I have given all I have
and you still will not love me,
I am coming on stumps to you, holding
out bouquets of these poor sunny feet and toes!

Love Song at the Olivetti on Fifth Avenue

Look, friends, at the tiny way
violets have in the grass—those
small blue bulbs that light its green:
windows of the dirt's cathedral,
skylights on the silences
and promises of the earth,
short stars a lawn mower threshes
into little heavens, falling
in the sun.
                    Come closer, friends;
I won't be long.
                              By actual count
there are, on any summer's day,
sixty-odd zentillion of them
(more than the real stars we see).
Right in our backyards!
our roadsides, friends, our fields and woods!
An incredible resource
since the dawn of time, these tiny flowers
have set their eyes on us,
from below; but we've been too
involved with wars and kings and things
to see that we can use them—
oh, not to eat, or wear, or burn
(though a salad would be good
shining with them, or icy-blue whiskey
in glasses tinted with their melted hue, jewels,
a rug fluffy as pollen
before a hearth, blue crackling petals
and pungent lights . . .). Technologists,
now the possibility
is pointed out, may make what they will.
I want no patent rights or royalties.

Here, somebody hold this sheet. Crowd in,
I'm nearly through.
                    My plan is easy,
to give, simply *give* them to each other—handfuls
of blue: cups, buckets, bushels, truckloads.
See them coming to market, mountains
of flowers piled in our streets and squares!
Think of the jobs! Think we could fight
wars with them, at a huge saving—
explosions not only like great flowers
but of a million flowers, showering
foxholes, fronts; or cities bombed
with their bright flakes, gay down of love—
and the bombers could stop for tea
before going back; everybody
laughing, talking, kissing in the streets; holding
out blue . . .
                    Please, somebody
nudge that lovely girl who's
yawning (I see her in the glass;
some people won't read anything if it's long).
Friends, I don't stand to make a penny;
I've come up from the country
to give the plan away for free,
like violets, or poems, or cash
(isn't she pretty, eyes like angels!)
so help yourselves (what I'm trying)
it's our world, after all
(to tell her is life is short
and I'll find her a violet and walk
her home hello hello

jjjjjjjjjjjjj

84

Hail and Farewell

Miss Debbie Newsonby taught Latin;
And wore her heart out, and her satin.

Hercynian elk and chesty legions
Primly roamed her mind's clear regions

Where aqueducts ran, and roads led always
Into Rome—as did our lockered hallways

To her shaded room: in which the Palatine
Matched its umbrellas of cypress and pine

(Open and shut) in a hairy wood,
And Castor's columns brokenly stood

Before the Senate (oak-framed of course),
And Mantegna's Caesar sat a horse.

She was Rome's future. As Rome taught
Barbarians by sword, she fought

Her yearly, wailing hordes with class sticks,
And dusty chalk, and periphrastics—

And won no more than Rome at last.
Like Rome, Miss Newsonby is past;

Felled amid her wriggling foemen,
Now dark she lies, a dainty Roman,

Ears stuffed to all the cries that dull us.
(What *did* she make of her Catullus?)

III

In a Spring Still Not Written Of

This morning
with a class of girls outdoors, I saw
how frail poems are
in a world burning up with flowers,
in which, overhead,
the great elms
—green, and tall—
stood carrying leaves in their arms.

The girls listened equally
to my drone, reading, and to the bees'
richocheting
among them for the blossom on the bone,
or gazed off at a distant mower's
astronomies of green
and clover, flashing,
threshing in the new, untarnished sunlight.

And all the while, dwindling,
tinier, the voices—Yeats, Marvell, Donne—
sank drowning
in a spring still not written of,
as only the sky
clear above the brick bell-tower
—blue, and white—
was shifting toward the hour.

Calm, indifferent, cross-legged
or on elbows half-lying in the grass—
how should the great dead
tell them of dying?

They will come to time for poems at last,
when they have found they are no more
the beautiful and young
all poems are for.

The Kite

Fearing branches,
    crash,
        tangled sticks

and paper in the end,
    the boy
        held

a red kite
    up, flashing,
        into the sky

of sunny March,
    up
        the mile-high towering

air,
    until it seemed
        an alien

speck in the peaceful heaven,
    parted
        from the tugging, disappearing

string. Occasionally,
    when the speck
        rolled

and was lost
    in the feathery sun,
        the dancing string

seemed, in his hand,
    a silvered line
        to pull him from the grassy

hill he stood on
    on
        into heaven.

For a moment
    it was possible,
        in such a world,

to trust forever in
    angels
        or the wind.

Saturday Movie

Daughter, within the darkened matinee
I watch you watch the colored forms invent
Dwarfs, prince, and girl—and the sorceress, intent
On doing her in to hear the mirror say
Herself most fair. Once, thirty years away,
In jeans, I blinked your tears and wonderment,
Leaning on the cushioned seat ahead, and bent
To the woody scene where sleeping Snow White lay—

As you behold, with blue eyes swimming bright,
The sweet undoing of the apple's charm,
The unriddling kiss—whose merely tinted light
I would weep for now, knowing an older harm
Must lead us out at last in the sun's hard sight:
An aging prince with innocence on his arm.

Steadfastness

The shining windy world we see impels
Illusion in us, keeps us seeing
Deepest constancies. As when water that rides
Loose in the bonds of its being
Sloshes out over the bucket's tin sides

Rather than betray its level earth-poise
For the abstraction of form;
Or the senseless twisting of a poplar leaf
Against the storm
That should make so frail a struggle brief.

We find love in the leaf for clinging fast,
Until we see it letting go
Gently, for no wind, its tiny-hoofed hold;
Have wonder for water so
Steadfast it scatters its crystal being and folds

To earth, until we've swung a sun-washed pail
Full round over our heads and seen
It ride the air. Oh well we know excess
Is never constant, light as any stone.
The heart cannot forgive such steadfastness.

Terror and Delight

Born to summer
he walked in a forest of dreams,
until that green world split
at all its seams,

and autumn drowned
and swept him in the mess of trees,
leaves bright and leaves brown.
But when the seas

of snow forgot
the hurt of dying things, he found
a kind of purity
in winter ground.

Distrusting green,
confusing terror and delight,
he died in the spring
with all his might.

What He Says

Raspberries splash, redly
    in their leaves;
        squirrels

squabble in the pine-tops.
    An old man,
        wearing

a sweater in warm July,
    breathes
        the same morning as the birds,

goes, talking among flowers
    beautiful as he is,
        bending,

leaves at his elbow.
    What he says,
        by himself, wandering

in the sunny garden,
    need not be true,
        nor useful.

Directions for Getting Lost

Since to take a walk means not to know
where you are going on it, you may
leave roads, plunge into woods after
a dangling-legged wasp, break spiders'
wires along a ferny path; or, ducking
a barbed-wire fence into sun, brush
a cornfield's rattling angels, try hills
that move the ground like an aerial view
too near your face, brambles like tracers
arching the way.

          But though a walk
means not to know where you are going,
you must be sure to know you've got there—
this is hardest. Something will tell you.
From a hill, seeing a half-hid town
glimpsed in branches, or looking down
rails endlessly arranging the fine distances,
or climbing a rise between hot fields
—in the whole wide emptiness of summer,
the road's edge starry with cornflowers, blue
as the eyes of girls . . . you'll know; know
to turn back here, or nowhere.

              You must not
have gone too far for coming back,
nor ever have gone farther than the daylight.
The ineffable must stay ineffable.
This is essential for you to learn,
not knowing how big a place death is
nor how many of the roads you see,
over horizons, may go there.

Omen

The big crows always come
before rain,
three of them; in the sunny pine,
or on the fence, among roses; somewhere.

We do not see them,
except then.
So far they have foretold
only the rain

with their cawings
—muddy fields
and the closed windows
at evening.

Above the River Country

Incredible
 as the tall moon is,
  lighting the fields above the river country,

its fencerows,
 and the shadowy woods
  through which the road

curves
 down to the sliding river,
  the silvered bridge under

which the river goes,
 light
  among the dark trees and rocks,

light in the dark leaves,
 beautiful:
  as you are.

O Bright Two

Two blue tinfoil Christmas angels tread
lightly, lightly, twisting on threads, the air
before the mantel mirror. They wear
golden haloes and golden wings.
Their skirts are satin blue. One of the pair,

six inches lower in its flight, swings
slowly, slowly, keeping watch; and overlooks
this shaded countryside of lamps, books,
the chairs, the pictured walls, and us.
Nearer the heaven where their threads have hooks

the other floats, higher, almost motionless;
motionless; enchants the chandelier
with painted looks among its sheer
crystal stars up near the ceiling.
In the round mantel mirror, they appear

their own twin angels. We wonder, being
two, two can find such perfect single grace,
moored from the ceiling. Their wooden faces
looking upward, red and white, are holy.
Weightless, they know their threaded places,

and build their simple heaven gaily there;
where they find themselves they find their stars,
these four-inch angels, until no world is far,
sure of love's endurance. O bright two,
O tell us clearly, truly, who we are.

A Last Photograph, for Being Divorced

Less love than that no one else can care
joins them, in this sea-dim kitchen light,
to that slimmer, smiling, earlier pair
who—were they wiser?—posed before
the glossily paneled, oak church door
or held the gleaming ship's rail tight.

Two shadows, wild hair in their eyes,
they lean to the mussed table sipping
bad dreams and coffee, hurt with surprise.
A cup of spoons makes iron flowers
of hopelessness, as in the thin dark hours
they sense what past it is they're slipping.

Hereafter strangers, they attend
the hour that keeps them, like story lovers
unable to go beyond *THE END*,
like Pip and Estella in their street,
who must unhappily meet
in the only scene now they'll have forever.

Girl in Front of the Bank

The windshield wipers clear an arc
in which you stand raincoated, blonde,
reshadowed on the bank's shiny glass

as you watch me. Your eyes are blue.
It's funny that a raincoat, belted,
buttoned, promises only you beneath—

as in a shift or woolen nightgown
sexier than lace. If lampposts (green)
were trees, I'd have you in the grass

and daisies—but here is all concrete.
No absolutes. Preparing to go off
into our separate lives, we are merely

by the moment's imagination
lovers, and see (we carefully look)
each other, with a fire, and glasses,

in shadowy chambers of the perfect grace.
We ignore what we might do
—wiser than Adam and Eve in flowers—

committed elsewhere, nowhere, longing.
I don't leap out. You wait your bus.
Yet, girl, we hold love's possibility.

Instructions for Keeping a Muse

Poems not written for love of a woman
rot, are dry, are crushed leaves already.
So let your poems be singing,
and your muse human,
not in robes, but in a skirt and sweater,
a slip, nothing.

Why should a man with only one life
(or a muse either)
bother with cold poems, distractions,
ideas: like tired men hunting a wife
and can't please her?
Love isn't abstractions.

See she knows she will be dead,
so her nipples harden
at your touch only, and her thighs stream
of the hot stars' milk and sperm.
Let her go down for it in street or garden
as fiercely as in bed.

Encounter

Hung within the weight of water
beneath the shadowy boathouse, masked,
from under the belly of a launch
I watch three fish hang like a mobile
over the weedy sand. Spotted, without words,
carefully distant, they watch me.
I am the wind that turns them slightly.
I am the stranger in this kingdom
so dim it won't hold shadows, or reflections.

Return

We came expecting gulls
circling in the white air,
geometers of a sunny town
that lies at the sea's edge
in the mind,
between the slow browns
of the land
and the endless blue,
the clumsy countryside
of the sea. So we come
always to our histories,
in the sunlight
at the broken edge of the sea
where sailboats turn,
bright, leaning.
                    Not
prepared ever for the road
empty and thin before us
—as it lay
in a nerveless rain;
the town, where we expected
the colors of flowers,
a sunless ruin
unpeopled in the pale rain.
And silent. The dock
where the leaded nets
dripped among the bales and boxes
lay dark and rotting
as if no sun
could lighten its sky;
masted and gloomy the boats,

that rode with the sun
when the sun rode with the sea
dancing and green,
swelled at their ropes.
Beyond its shattered rocks
the sea fumbled
itself, slick and gray, moving
the leaden wingless gulls
on their bobbing, tumbled
heaven.
        Only love
ever
stretching outward as the sea
stretches outward to sun-filled scenes
beyond this difficult sky,
can find gulls flying
in the white air
in sunlight,
the fleecing boats slim
on the earth's edge,
beyond this dying weather.

Among the Finger Lakes

These great brown hills move in herds, humped like bison,
before the travelling eye. Massive above the farms, they file
and hulk daylong across every distance; and bending come
as the sun sinks (orange and small) beyond their heavy
       shoulders,
shaggy at evening, to drink among the shadowy lakes.

The Two Roads

The old road runs along by the new
Behind a space of weeds and alders,
But, occasionally forgetful, falters
Up a hill the turnpike arrows through;

Or, bending, wanders unwinding out
Across the summer country's flowing,
As if not sure of where it's going,
At least preferring to go roundabout,

—Being off to find a wood, or hunt
Some crossroads' single clapboard store
Which hides behind its blown screen door
A scented coolness, guarded in front

By one gas-pump; or to thread a town
Too small and distant to be picked
To be a suburb ever, its brick
And burnt-out bank-shell going down

Slowly, filled up with grassy weeds
And treelings leaning out at windows
And at ghostly doors that never close,
Its houses gray with unwieldy needs

In the sun. Then, rising to view
Over a far-off ridge, the old black-
Top comes loyally struggling back
And runs a length beside the new

—Before, ducking under and astray,
It goes off to collect perhaps
A pretty creek that greenly laps
Its grasses, or a field a mile away

Where last month's hooded lightning fell;
A house you might stop at for eggs
Or corn, or just to stretch your legs
And pump a cold drink up from the well

Beneath the tall elm-shade, or toss
(Or wish to toss) a stone up, waiting
By the car, to make the phone wires sing
Before going on. Two highways cross,

Recross, the sunny black, the silver,
And, sharing all the country, stride
Rivers on bridges side by side,
And graph the summer's green together.

Under the September Peach

A hundred ruddy peach-moons ring the grass,
dark-jewelled with wasps, in whose oppressive hum
the dark machinery of ruin runs
in the sunny garden. Full half of summer's weight,

they gaze like desolate mirrors up into
the leafy heaven of the tree, where still
a hundred yellow-reddening planets swing
a zodiac, loose upon the strings of space,

—and fall, by ones and twos, into this round
and glittering junkyard of the summer's air,
low circle of a spilled Hesperides:

whose tiny dragons gorge the rusting fruit,
and peer, like eyes, from angry eaten caves
of sweetness, up, to see the still unfallen sky.

Municipal Parking Lot

Safe, lunar in its spiny fence,
the township's
nightly dome of humming arc light blooms,
glows—cannibal of shadows,

a froth of stony blues. Two beat-up
Plymouths,
caught in the jewely fungus, hang
like beetle hulks among the stars.

Ghosts

The rain
    of the deep middle night
        hangs

steadily in the trees,
    dark,
        amid the lightless heavy leaves,

and settles
    down black suburban streets and lawns.
        My townsmen sleep

deep among their sleeping wives,
    dreaming Eden,
        in a pretty town

where ghosts alone
    would watch from darkened windows
        on the rain,

or wait the dangling hours out
    to see
        the streetlamp's yellow

tin-reflector-petaled flower
    pale
        at last upon its corner stem.

One January

At the full of summer the spider swung
His net against the wind, and anchored it
From the morning-glory vines and the white
Corner of the garage, and in the full sun

Plied his precarious trade all summer long,
And in October disappeared. But his web,
Like a torn and impossible memory,
Has clung to its slender moorings, and hung

Derelict and storm-battered on; and
This morning boasts a dry brown leaf flung
There through the night by some quick wind,
A meager glory for the coming year.

The House

I had seen it all year, but had never
gone to it. From my telephone window
it seemed a shed, on the far slope where my
neighbor's pasture backs against his pinewoods;
it took a sunny winter day, beginning thaw,
to get me there to find it was a house,
or had been a house once, and after that
a shed for storing hay, and then a house
again but, empty, only for children
to play in until the floor boards started
to sag, crack open, and it seemed unsafe
even for that. After forty years it
had taken a decided tilt, and leaned
out backward from the top so that even
the doorways (doorless) were askew as if
to welcome only slanted men. Flat, brown, the stones
on which it sat, at corners and beneath
the doors, were crooked legs, that walked it
crazily into the light.
                    My neighbor,
having seen me, came along to see what
I was up to, bringing as his excuse
a bucket of seeds for the thaw to work
into the frost-puffed ground, and told me such
little as he knew about the house. The tin
roof, now red-brown with rust, had been put on
when his predecessor kept his hay stuffed
there; he himself had nailed the single planks
to the doorways, to keep the children out
(they didn't look as if they could have); and
he supposed he would have to pull it down
some year, if the weather didn't save him

that. He made sure I saw the axe marks on
the six-inch timbers, in between which, cracked
dry as lines of an old face, the mud was
falling out in little cubes; and left me
(being sure I wasn't up to anything)
to have the place to myself.

                          Inside, up
over the stepless sill and past his plank,
I stood gingerly on the sagging, torn
floor boards, still littered with a wash of straw
gray as cobwebs. The chimney was falling
in on itself, the upper stones tumbled
like a stone sock turning inside out, with
a toe of brown rocks spilled from the fireplace
onto the floor. And arching vines, green-coined
even in winter, stretched their suckers in
the windows, in the edges of the hole
where a corner gaped wide as if the house
had thought of a picture window by itself
(a good view of the valley: sentinel
spruces dark against the ochre grasses,
wire fences in a wild geometry
up to the road, and woods on the far rise).
The other room, back of the stairway, must
have been the kitchen, but was bare, the sun
illuminating the gray walls on which
the daubers had hung panpipes of red mud,
stiff, musical, in an empty house.

                          The high
rotted stairs let me peek at the loft-rooms,
a half-wall between them, the tin roof smoke-
colored on its underside. Both ends were
open—cones among the green needles on
the woods-end, ten feet away from the house,
and only cold sky through the other end,

from which the chimney had melted, twisting
the wallboards into a splintery screen
through which the snow must have piled darkly nights
when no one was watching skies from the house,
no valley lights visible. The vines had
invited themselves in, summer nights, days,
when no one was using the loft, and left
a tracery of color to match the pines
at the other open end.
                I got back down,
lit a cigaret, and settled myself among
the furniture of stones and curling vines
to watch, beyond my frosting breath, the view
from the picture window. I didn't feel
I was trespassing on the former owners,
whoever they had been, by taking their
cozy fireside for my bright afternoon;
all houses come to this, and even pity
could not imagine their evenings, tiny
now at the far end of time's telescope,
beside a real fire in this old room,
nor love intrude on abandoned privacies
of talk over a table, of pride on
summer mornings, of loneliness at windows.
They may have had good reasons for leaving
—even dying could have been—but they are
beyond our intentions, dim, strange, cryptic.
What we can read is, not them, but this rune
of wood, of old stone. It was the house, still,
colorful with the flavors of itself,
purged of its uses, that rode out the cold,
the winds, like an old ark, cheery, having
forgotten what it once had had a mind to save.
The thing I felt was clarity, not love.
My truth was all the hardiness of a house,

the way the wood and stone, having taken
a shape, refused to give it up—like poems
taken into newer centuries, tilted to
alien weathers, refusing to go down,
sharp, buoyant, queer. Not the people of
the house, the loss; but the made-thing
itself, forgetting them, which kept a stance they
once gave it, and never would be as it might
have been without them. What stays, not what goes.
A lastingness.
           Across the thawing fields
I saw my house, not even built when this
first touched its prow against the swelling green
of Virginia hills; my puppy, bouncing
in the yard, was a white spot beside the car.
A hardiness.
           That open shade, vine-browed,
was like an eye from which I looked across
to my own life, a yard I had not tended
well enough—the puppy's clutter of rags
and bones and plastic bottles dotting it—;
my blood ran clearer in my wrists, sight
in my eyes. My hands were hungry for the tools
by which such alien things, houses, verses,
are made to take a landscape by the pure
idea turned to stone or wood or words,
and are left haunting the wind's tingling, clumsy ear
or tempting its slow touch to pull down walls
sharper than such windy fingers.
                        I took
my grassy path back to the present, took
up my life as if I'd never been away,
the puppy jumping at me as I came,
the raggy stuff of zinnias crackling in wind
by the porch, eave-shadows on the windows

I would look out of. I made the porch-boards thump,
in sun, as if I'd never been away
—except for sensing that ragged eye I'd
been inside of, watching me, from a hill
facing the slope I'd set my living on.

From My Window at the College

I am a man, at a window
through which the February sunlight falls,
warmth through glass;
and I look, from the window, on a prospect
of fields and woods. Nearest,

in the ridges of contoured, dark-red earth,
a pasture being remade,
lie melting feathers of the snow
that leaped the mountains in the night
and flew seaward, while we all were sleeping.

I would say good things of the earth, the day.
Some have loved me,
I have loved some; the branch, in the gray thicket
at the hidden foot of the slope,
is running clear, channeled in borders of ice.

The year strains upward. I make my eyes
put green to all I see, the light, the trees, the grass;
fires kindle into nothingness.
The landscape is the landscape that I see.
The sun remains a radiant wheel.

A fly is with me at the window.
Launching from the glass, he makes a dizzy celebration
on the sill, drops, lies, legs up
as if he were walking the wind;
and rights himself. The present is an endless country,

of which those woods like a sea of arrows
stretching to the end of what I see
make but a portion. Such dry colors,
bare woods, fields, winter fences,
in lines and patterns, are the architecture

of the spring, steel leaves not more enduring
than leaves that vanish.
I shall not stop the closing of the light;
and if I would, the stars, already
there, upon their silver bush around my head,

would hang their twiggy lights in every eye.
Now, surely, only, it is afternoon.
The horses of the light romp in endless gallop;
stones, clouds, and trees. In the end,
Orestes became friendly with the Furies.

I see the world as if in water. Beyond the midnight lamp,
the bed and girl, the daylight
moves in its enormous stillness along the hills.
All that is, is forever.
No memory, illusion, wrecks the world

where sheets of wind are bending the light around.
A bluff of pines, solid
as a wave, hard as the color of the sea,
takes shadows on its front.
A tiny fence, beneath a stride of distant poles,

carries a hidden road on which no figures travel.
A man crossing a field
would people the world again, but he doesn't come.
Even a bird, a hawk
about some business from the hills, drifting,

would seed the vision of the lidless light,
a jewel, reduced to ashes.
The winter branches arch, in love, and leaves
are rising like pulses through the blood;
hurt stirs its green wings in the bud.

I would say good things of the earth, the day,
and of those I love.
Spring is not yet. But in brightening grayness,
in this metal springtime, there is more love
than we could realize in a field of flowers.